Lost in the White Ruins

Lost in the White Ruins

William Walsh

© 2014 William Walsh All rights reserved. This material may not be reproduced in any form, published, reprinted, recorded, performed, broadcast, rewritten or redistributed without explicit permission of William Walsh. All such actions are strictly prohibited by law.

Any resemblance to actual people (living or dead), events, or locales is entirely coincidental. The names, characters, places, and incidents in these poems are the product of the author's imagination.

ISBN 13:978-0692225493

Kelsay Books
Aldrich Press
www.kelsaybooks.com

—in memory of my father

*who taught me to play baseball
and to get back up
when the world
knocked me down*

Many thanks to my friends and teachers who read early versions of these poems: Julie E. Bloemeke, David Bottoms, Fred Chappell, Beth Gylys, Henry Hart, Kevin Meaux, Mike Saye, Megan Sexton, Leon Stokesbury, and John Williams. I am indebted.

Contents

I. Wild Wreckage

Hunting Mule Deer	13
Reading from the *Portuguese* in Atikokan	17
Thoughts During a Thunderstorm: Montana	19
The Old Me	21
Betrayal	23
Feeling Like I'm in a William Holden Movie	24
My Last Fishing Trip	28
Outside Winn Dixie in Suburban Plaza	30
Hero with a Thousand Faces	31

II. When Beauty Obscures Reasoning

Spoon River in Uganda	41
Blackbird	42
Elegy for a School Bus Driver	44
Friday, Before Dusk	46
Lake Lure	47
Ownership	49
The *Uncertainty Principle*	50
Thomas Merton, Womanizer, Contemplates Our Future	51
Sister Mary Armageddon Teaches Her Students to Hold a Grudge at Saint John of the Impossible Elementary School on 7th Street	52
Skating on Maud's Pond	53

III. Family Matters

First Taste of Salt	57
The Big Cat Tracks My Grandfather	61
Scrabble at 8:00 P.M.	62
Erie, PA 1969: The Night My Father was Pick-Pocketed	63

My Mother Almost Becomes Friends with Ann-Margret	65
Jon, Age Eleven	67
The Last House on the Left	68
Skating on Chautauqua Lake, 1920s	69
My Grandfather's Christmas Tree	70
When the Bowling Ball Flew Through the T.V.	71
Come Fly with Me	72
My Daughter Likes to Fly	74
A Path to Elk Creek	76
Snazzy Pants on Valley Road	77
In Celebration of Roy Orbison's Birthday	78
Homage: For My Father	80

IV. A Tow-Line of Barbed-Wire

The Movie Star's Secret	84

Acknowledgements
Notes
About the Author

I. Wild Wreckage

Drunk on the wind in my mouth,
Wringing the handlebar for speed,
Wild to be wreckage forever.

—James Dickey

Hunting Mule Deer

The fall I turned seven, a year before my daddy was murdered,
he took me hunting with his best friend, Gus Reynolds,
beyond forty miles of cane-break in West Texas
on property owned by a football coach Gus knew
from his playing days. With a cooler full of *Cokes*,

long-neck bottles of *Lone Star*, and a gunny sack
of sandwiches, we drove two hours
beyond Odessa to the coach's ranch
to hunt his land. If not, Gus said, he knew another spot.
It was my first time hanging out with Gus
and listening to my father talk about work, "Anything you hear
from up here, you don't repeat." When we arrived,

Gus told daddy to stay put riding shotgun.
He had to smooth out a few things still lingering
from his last visit, but was pretty certain his invitation
was still open to hunt the old man's property.
Gus and I walked up to the porch
since the old man had a soft spot for kids
with no front teeth and bad haircuts. When Gus knocked

on the front door, the coach stepped onto the porch
and said he'd be more than happy to let us hunt, but first
Gus needed to do him a favor. "See that old mule

standing by the barn?" he said, pointing to a skinny jackstock.
"I've had that mule for nearly thirty years. He's sick
an' in a lot of pain, an' I just can't bring myself to shoot 'em.
Gus, would you shoot my mule?"

"Coach, I'd rather not shoot your mule. I'll mend fences,
shuck corn, brand cattle. I'll do whatever I can,
but I'd rather not shoot that mule."

"I unnerstand, but my wife and daughter are away
shopping and it'd be the greatest favor
you could do for me while they're gone.
I'd do it myself, but it's like shooting a favorite dog
or your mother-in-law."

I stood looking up to both men.
"Seeing how you've been so generous
to me all these years,
okay, I'll do it. I'll shoot your mule."

"Young feller, you ever been hunting?" he asked me.
I shook my head no. As Gus and I walked back to his station wagon,
he said, "I'm gonna play a joke on your daddy."
I thought, "Okay."

Gus slammed the car door shut and pounded on the steering wheel.
"What's wrong?" my old man asked him.

"That son of a bitch told me to get the hell off his property,
that we couldn't hunt
and that I was the sorriest football player
he ever coached in his entire life
and you weren't much better. He wondered
how the hell the F.B.I. ever hired you,
because you're so stupid
you couldn't hit the ground if you fell out of an airplane."

"He said that?"

"Sure as hell did."

"He don't hardly know me. I ain't met the man
but once," my daddy said, shaking his head.

"I'm gonna fix his ass. Boy, git out here with me."
Gus jumped out of the driver's seat, leaned into the window
at my father and pointed to the man's mule.

"You see that mule?
I'm gonna kill that son of a bitch's mule."

He high-tailed it around to the tailgate
and grabbed his shotgun.
I trailed behind. He winked at me
then loaded one round, cocked his rifle, set the sights,
and as the mule lowered his head to eat a snip of alfalfa,
"Bam!" One shot through the neck and the mule fell over
with a peaceful thud.

I was too scared to look at my daddy.
I felt bad for the mule.
Gus just stood there
milking this for all it was worth, staring off
at the dead mule as if he had just laid down
a pronghorn antelope with a bow.
Then as I took a deep breath, *"Bam! Bam!"*
my old man had his 30-30 shoulder-locked.
He turned and looked toward Gus.
"I just got two of his cows,
let's get the hell out of here."

Reading from the *Portuguese* in Atikokan

Walking through an Ontario forest to a field of cord grass,
swaying, circular, as I sat on my moss mat, reading,
overlooking Batchewaung Bay,
I wondered why the world fails to explain
how nothing first becomes something,
like a woman's love for a man or the spark
of an idea to create anything, say a poem
or song or painting. It is an act of faith
to create, to believe beyond mere existence,
yet, before us, nearly inexplicably, the world unfolds
like a *Nodding Trillium*.

It is faith these Boy Scouts have that I can lead them
into the wilderness and out safely, sixty miles
from the nearest road. Faith is a dangerous land
filled with bear, rutting moose, open water
lightning storms, but in time, we succumb to the idea
of pulling a mystery from the depths
as our lures scour the boney waters.
I can call it nothing else as we stick our hands
through the universe, like the *Hubble* telescope,
to the other side for His, unsure what is out there.
We never know much about the world
until we must explain it to our children.

Then, canoeing to Lake Agnes to the petroglyphs,
with my line dragging behind the stern,
I thought of the man 20,000 years ago
who drew bison, deer, and an auroch,
painted his hand on the wall in red ochre
then left. Did he think about the stars?
What would he have thought about the fire I built
this evening, the blue walleye sizzling on the spit
and the stories we told, and how we've come to believe
in what we cannot see or know, including ourselves.

Thoughts During a Thunderstorm: Montana

There are no yesterdays
when traveling alone, no concerns
as you drive by empty factories, rusted
grain silos, alfalfa fields, and miles
of white-line fever when you're running
from whatever curls your haunting
into a hollow shell.

You can be whomever you decide to be at *IHOP*
or sitting in a dusty bus station,
telling the next stranger a new history.
I told her my name was Robert.
She was Iris, but I'll bet
it was probably Debbie or Jennifer
as she wrote down her cell number,
squeezing her mauve suitcase between her feet
then reading an old travel magazine, pretending
to be from Bozeman.

Where you are right now
is where you are. There is no one
to hold the past against you
as you zip by mileage markers
in a rented *Ford Escort*
with time to think about women

you've kissed, ones you never laid
down in a dried field, the cool wind
as fresh as a new baseball,
the tack-leather smell you almost want to taste.

On the road, your history is some waitress's greasy plate
as you head out, leaving the old world behind
like unpaid bills, some hastily-ended relationships
kicking up gravel in the street as the engine howls
for attention. My waitress's name is Rosemary.
This time I'm Stan.

There's always a girl like Iris in a small cow town
who says to call if you're ever in Seattle.
And there's always a crossroad
without directional markers as you sit alone
in your car looking east, then west, hail
pinging out *Morse* code on the roof top,
tapping out your future.

The Old Me

Tuesday there was a knock on the front door
that broke up my marriage with the mattress.
I felt compelled to answer
and there I was standing on the other side
of the door
through expensive cut glass
but thirty years younger.

Stepping outside to welcome
my 20/20 vision back where it belonged,
the younger me
threw a pie in my old face
then ran down the street
hooting and hollering
shedding articles
of clothing until all I saw
was the firm
naked butt of a guy
I hardly remember.

He was much faster
but still, I ran after him
with chunks of pie falling
off my face (at least he remembered
peach) and I yelled out to him, "Wait!
There's so much I need to tell you
and what you can expect, especially
that girl from New Mexico."

But he did not stop
and I don't think he was listening.

Down the street
there was a beautiful young girl
running naked toward him,
her light brown hair
flowing everywhere.
And running behind her, an old bag
of a woman I slightly recognized.

The younger me drove off
with the younger her
in a yellow *Volkswagen*
convertible, Night Ranger
blaring out "Sister Christian"
from a new pair of speakers.

"Take me with you," I yelled.

Her hand gripped the knob
of the stick shift
and as he clutched,
she shifted gears
for him in perfect
automotive harmony.

They were laughing
—not at me—
but for the future.

Betrayal

I could tell she liked me by how often she returned to my table
with fresh coffee and willing small talk, standing a little too close

for a married woman, and maybe if I had pressed the issue
I could have pushed for something more, gained her confidence

as some men do with a woman
who steps through the world unnoticed

except when pirouetting plates of bacon and grits.
As a detective, I noticed everything: her jeans cutting low

on her ashen hips, the Democrat bumper stickers
on her *Prius*, the hoop earrings and lipstick

she put on after I arrived, new *Rebox*,
a $200 *Fossil* watch—a Christmas gift from her husband

three years ago—and how she comped my breakfast
after I said she had beautiful blue eyes

even though they were green. Because,
as I moved through the darkness of my shadow

like a Cold War spy, breath heaving against the boredom
of an ordinary life, she sat down at my table

and asked what it's like being colorblind.
She told me everything I wanted to know about her life,

smiling that a stranger could be so fascinating.
Then I asked her a question. And another.

Feeling Like I'm in a William Holden Movie

The woman across the street is sexy
but volatile, like a .45 revolver

sitting on the coffee table—you don't dare
grab it too quickly. I bet she walks

around the house naked, drinking
Martini Five-Os in the afternoon.

Sometimes around midnight, I hear her
screaming at him. I've watched her

chuck baskets of clean clothes
out the upstairs window, their passion

floating like rider-less parachutes
exploding on the lawn, his shoes

tumbling into the street.
She might be the answer

to all that seems wrong
in a man's life, in my life,

but I can't stop dreaming about her.
She's as nice as a stray cat, then

a soft hiss, an explosion
like the *Mont-Blanc* that leveled

Halifax, Nova Scotia in 1917.
And maybe, if I just saw her naked

once, my curiosity, my desire,
would fade. Perhaps

I'll grow a goatee. Or, maybe
if I could just touch her

deeply with my poems
her body would hum

a different tune.
He drinks too much, always

wants to take me to a strip club, always
tells me what he figures I don't know

and borrows from my tool shed
whatever he doesn't feel like buying.

It's a law as constant as gravity:
if he wants her, he can't have her,

and if she wants him to agree
with her opinion, he disagrees

just to annoy her. In all honesty,
she's not the kind of woman I'm looking for,

but no matter how pleasant he tries
to be, I want to bash him in the head

with a hammer, snatch her up
then call him on the phone

at two a.m.: "Guess what?
Super Hero Soup

and burnt toast! I want
to marry Jenny Lou."

An hour later, after he's
eased back into a comfortable

R.E.M. dream, I call again,
"Lard casserole with grape *Kool-Aid*.

I've tied the house down
with ropes." He yells,

"Just keep her!" and slams
the phone in my ear. . .

. . . and there she is
in my cream-colored oxford

button-down shirt, legs
curled up to her chest

in my leather chair, sexy
in her flowered underwear,

sipping a cup of herbal tea,
her brown hair bouncing

off her shoulders, green eyes
of cat-glow purring, "What now,

Pussycat?" . . . and I think,
Ann-Margret, and I wonder, too,

"Now what?" — but know
her cotton panties

are just minutes from circling
her left ankle. . . .

In the background of our new life
Jackie Brenston and His Delta Cats

tickle the ivory of "Rocket 88."
The weather outside is calm.

Then, through the window—a tuft
of breeze, a wisp of air

begins to slightly move
behind the curtains.

My Last Fishing Trip

En route to Colorado for a final getaway
to Climax, Dinosaur, or Hygiene,

towns where I could easily cast myself into
a jon boat and fish for something

the depths hold secret,
I wanted to call and say I'd given up

on the idea Elvis might be living
or that our marriage would scab over

while I was gone. What I found was
Hammond, Louisiana, the sweaty crotch

of the U.S.A., its legion of cavemen
and three-hour pizza delivery.

Charlie Rich never expected to die
in this rancid alligator back-wash, and yet,

there I was in room 109 at the *Holiday Inn*,
Charlie's last stop, calling a repair shop

for a busted transaxle and fluid leaking
from the underbelly of my truck.

All I wanted was to move forward
toward some moment in life

where family is proud for the good
work I've done. Whatever

the world did not want me to find,
I never found in Hammond, say, for instance,

happiness, or a few bucks tucked in my back pocket,
or *the* girl with two answers: *yes* and *maybe*. Something

as good as that. Stranded with few options
and toting the weight of pink slips, past due notices,

and a process server trying to track me down,
even Last Chance, Colorado whispered *there's hope*

that a boat can drift across God's mountain lake
exactly the way a bowling ball can't.

Outside Winn Dixie in Suburban Plaza

Late Saturday night, 1986, and again I had no one
to hang out with, just a few poems
and a notion of what to do, when I saw a girl
not much older than sixteen in the back of a car
under the drunken parking lot lights,
her eyes watered-down with a slacked milky glaze,
full of what I knew must be her childhood
being pushed off a north Georgia cliff by two boys
running into *Winn Dixie* for more *P.B.R.*

After more than twenty years, I like to think I've helped
enough people along the way to quiet my regret,
repaired the heavy elegy I carry on my back
for my father and what he might say,
"Never leave a stranger stranded."

As I walk through my house, I check the locks
on each door, turn off the lights, the t.v., the gas logs,
then up stairs to the hall and around a pile of *Legos*
left on the floor. I step lightly to each child's room,
place a train on the dresser, adjust the bed covers,
tuck a bear under an arm, turn off a closet light.
Each cheek is dry to my kiss. Room to room,
I make my rounds like a doctor or maybe like Superman
spinning the earth backwards to save Lois Lane.

Hero with a Thousand Faces

In California, there's a woman named Marilyn Monroe
which makes me wonder what her life must be like, if perhaps
she has movie-star beauty or maybe she's a mother

touring her children around the city to baseball games
and piano practice. I'm pretty certain she must be tired
of the old jokes— "You don't look anything like her,"

from every grocery store clerk, bank teller,
or department store saleswoman—what must she endure
on a first date, the undeliverable expectations,

the presumptuous ogling of the male libido, the sexiness
of a dream-film played over in a guy's mind,
the wanton playfulness, and everyone insisting she sing

at every birthday party like a lap dance for JFK,
or even the simple task of buying a pair of shoes or pantyhose
or having the oil changed at Red's Service Station.

She never hears the whispered stories after she's left
the photography studio with her children, and the photographer,
with a clip-on tie and short-sleeved shirt from *Wal-Mart*,

brags to his D&D online friends as though he were George Barris
rattling off black and white beach scenes of Marilyn,
barefooted and wrapped in a thick wool sweater

and Bermuda shorts, a fantasy
Christmas present ready to be opened.
In Nevada, there's one—a Marilyn Monroe

for some other man's fantasy at the end of the day,
and another in Hawaii and thirty-four Marilyns
throughout the South. There are seven Ronald Reagans

in California. Eighteen Bob Barkers, three Johnny Carsons,
three Don Knotts, and a dozen Andy Taylors—no mention
if any have been sheriff. Martha Washington lives on

Washington Avenue, no doubt the most famous person
in El Monte, California. William Faulkner, 150 in the US (good luck
with that novel), especially the four guys in Mississippi

and the poor slob hanging his hat in Sardis,
that little postage stamp of grief
every time he walks into the library or *Barnes & Noble*.

There are two E. Hemingways scattered on the West Coast,
and by virtue of the fact that they use *E*
I'll wager we know who they really are.

I try to imagine the comedic scene, envision the trouble,
they have buying a shotgun in deer season. And George
Machine Gun Kelly, your name is splattered across America

like the spray from a Tommy gun. Twelve Elizabeth Bishops
(perhaps one's jotting down a grocery list in verse—
Shakespearean couplets—or trying to rhyme *cantaloupe*

against her feelings and the burden of societal expectations
while her daughter burns her *Barbie* dolls
in effigy) but tonight, Betsy Bishop's energy is turned

towards preparing dinner. Of the more than two dozen
Emily Dickinsons—I wonder
if the sweet woman in Amherst, Massachusetts

is stewing in her attic or is she really from Topeka
and moved to Amherst for some odd recognition
or maybe she has a great sense of humor

and wears black and is frigid
and tells everyone who comments on her name
that when she dies she will be the fly buzzing in their ear.

Throughout the country there are over fifty Barney Fifes,
two in North Carolina—how many times do you think
one of them has walked into a barber shop

only to hear, "Hey, Barney,
Thelma Lou's looking for you." Then there's
William Walsh, the 16th Century poet, who's made it tough

for me because I cannot even claim my name in verse
as original, or in San Francisco
where twenty-two men are pretending to be me.

Maybe they'll be some flowery fellows riding
skateboards down Lombard Street or the *49ers*
football coach—I've never heard that before.

"He's my father," I say to make people feel stupid.
If I could be someone else, I would. I'd change everything
about me—my name, hair color, style,

height, skin tone, accent, fat-to-muscle ratio—I'd
compile myself into a suave man among men, Paul Newman
(eight in Georgia) and with my new costume,

I'd drive to West Liberty, Kentucky in my '57 *Corvette* to propose
to Joanne Woodward, to change our lives together—we could
be anyone from anywhere, but she'd have to go for it, go all out,

completely change, like me, and learn a new language, because
who I really want to be is Eduardo Masso
with a personality that could sway any woman

into my arms with exotic romantic syllables sashaying
from my tongue—I'd learn Portuguese and while standing
on a balcony overlooking Rio de Janeiro, I'd kiss the nape of her neck

while her hair flowed backwards in the wind. Yes, I would
become him and he would be me. I'd need to learn Spanish, too,
because I have no formal training

other than *Speedy Gonzales* cartoons and an eighth grade girlfriend
who really knew how to kiss but her brother didn't
like gringos and scared me off with a large knife

he held under my right ear. I can sympathize
with the guy in Florida named Theodore Bundy.
Maybe he lives alone in a trailer on a dirt road

just to get away from the mailbox smashing
and prank phone calls. There are fifteen
William Walshes in Georgia, 130

in the south alone, and one guy in Kentucky
with my exact name, William John Walsh, III.
There's another in New Jersey and Massachusetts—

just like me—the exact same name. But it's not me!
I hope they're illiterate. I hope
they wouldn't know a poem from a brick bat.

At least I have that over them. Maybe
the government can make the written driving test
a sonnet essay. I would shine above those guys!

There are so many William Walshes
on the eastern seacoast, I stay away
because in all probability

there's an outstanding felony arrest warrant
for one of them. But it's not me. So now, I've decided
I want to be Eduardo Masso because there are no

Eduardo Masso men anywhere—maybe
I can be the only one, be free
from the fear of running into myself

at a sloppy topless bar, nursing
a few shots of *Jose Cuervo*
or in a police lineup, be free

from the other guy, the guilty
William Walsh, the one pointing
his finger at me—can't they see

that I'm clean shaven and he's grungy
and the police arrested him peeing in an alley
behind a *CVS* drugstore

and when they came for me in the library
I was researching Joseph Campbell
and the different masks we wear, when a cop

threw me on the floor like a literary hog
and held his boot to the back of my neck?
And yes, I'm quite likely to argue

with the cops and give them the damnedest time
about never having been to Bangor, Maine,
and having no idea how to rob a bank

and yeah, I know all about the child molester in a Georgia prison
with my name and same general height
and weight characteristics, but it's not me,

and if it were legal—or if I had the remote chance
of getting away with it—I'd shoot the son of a bitch myself—just wait
in the woods with a high-powered rifle and *Gemtech* silencer

for when he's standing in the yard
at the foul line ready to toss up a free-throw
through the net-less hoop. First, I would unload

on the basketball, have him wondering
what just happened and then as he was bending over
examining the splintered rubber sphere—one shot,

one fewer William Walsh. When the police
pulled me up from the library floor, cuffs too tight around my wrists,
there's always one smart-ass cop who tries to tell me

something he thinks I don't know—I tell him
I have only one mask that I wear before he smashes me in the face
with the butt of his rifle. "Here's a black eye for that mask."

Now, I remember, Eduardo Masso, the improved man
I want to become, the savior of myself, the *new-to-the-job* me,
the changeling bad boy turned good,

inside, lurking somewhere,
but there's already a man
named Eduardo Masso, a tennis player

from Argentina—a man I should have remembered,
who played Jimmy Connors twenty years ago
at the *AT&T* tournament. I sat in the fourth row

center net, and though I loved Connors,
the gritty hero, I cheered for Masso, the southpaw
with Adonis hair, because, really,

would one more victory have changed
Jimmy Connors's life? But what it would have done
for Eduardo Masso, and me,

to defeat the greatest—we could have
been something. So, here I am
on a Thursday, the winter chill

beginning to lift on a rainy afternoon, and I'm thinking
about my parents and how I want
a new name, a new identity, and why

they didn't have the forethought to bless me
with originality, because now all I really want
is to be Eduardo Masso with wild wreckage hair

bouncing and flowing with abandon
into a new life, the sexy swagger of confidence
of the man I really should have been

all my life, into the only life I have been given,
name and all, a crude history
dragging behind me.

There are times when I don't feel so awful
because out there scattered across the country
are 648 George Washingtons with a legacy they cannot live up to,

none having crossed any river
of significance into anything new or worthy
of remembrance, undetermined to be anything

other than who they really are.
I am simply me, this guy with a life,
a story that is nothing to brag about

but at times good enough, just a guy
who signs the back of a paycheck
with a signature indecipherable as anyone's life.

II. When Beauty Obscures Reasoning

Dead riches, dead hands, the moon
Darkens,
And I am lost in the beautiful white ruins
Of America.

—James Wright

Spoon River in Uganda

On the road from Kampala, the air was heavy
as jack fruit when we left Fort Portal, twelve hours
of ruts and dust to watch elephants.
It was only me and the bus driver (Moses) awake
in the darkness, chewing sugar cane
and gnawing roasted goat
from the night before. The sulfur smell
from the Lake Katwe salt mines
gave me a headache. Cab light weak,
I read a poem by a man now dead, his distant epistle
radio-ing an important message
from somewhere, like the letter I wrote my grandfather
in 1990, returning to me two months ago
after my aunt sifted though his desk
for insurance papers. To hold on to my letter
all these years—I wasn't quite sure
what to make of it. Maybe it was the last letter I wrote to him
before cheap long-distance, or maybe,
like a poem, he occasionally read it
to hear my voice. Then at five-thirty in the morning,
with no bota-bota cutting us off in traffic,
as Moses negotiated a slight curve
on a country road, a leopard crossed my path.

Blackbird

Sure—
I will read

her poem
but it hurts

to the bone
to find her here

in such fine pages
like the time

I found her
wrinkled in linen

with her teacher
as I stood

over them
the sleep-smell

of sex
emptying from her

how I wanted
to lasso his twins

with a shoestring
and slam the door shut

but instead
I read a poem

about his wife
from his debut

until he woke
and ran

down the street
his clothes clutched

to his chest like a stack
of loose twenties.

It's simply amazing
how some people

are frightened
by a 12-gauge

sense of humor.
The arched back

of fog
whiskers through

the night as
I feel my skin

strangely
warmed

by this darkness
touching

my heart
under my

clothes.
Her beauty

obscures
my reasoning.

Elegy for a School Bus Driver

Because my daughter needed bubble wrap
for a science project, and because

we popped all of them
in the car before we got home,

I drove back to *Publix*
where I also bought a Sunday paper

and found Palmer Beck's photograph.
While Olivia squatted on top of the kitchen table

in her bare feet, carefully
gluing macaroni to a blue poster board,

I laid down my last summer
of baseball to memory—how he stood alone,

away from the other parents, his fingers
gripping the chain-link fence, black lines

of grime half-circling beneath his nails—angel
of the grease rack watching his gangly son

fall backwards in right field
as a *can of corn* arced overhead.

With real skin in the game,
minor league scouts charted my pitches,

but it wasn't my slow curve that eventually caused the trouble,
it was my Vida Blue snowball slipping one winter morning

at the bus stop, off just enough
to catch Connie under her wire-rimmed glasses,

exploding like a depth charge
of bitchiness. Crying, she ratted me out.

As he looked up through the oblong mirror
to where I sat quietly on the back row, ready

for whatever another day of detention might bring,
somehow I was spared by a man who knew

how it was to be stuck in a mill town
with no escape plan.

Friday, Before Dusk

Chipping golf balls into the cemetery
behind my house, a sand wedge

to the Virgin Mary, I heard a rodeo
of scraping, a pack of rats scuffling

on the gravel, gnawing one of their own.
A handful of stones scattered them

to leave the wounded one to die
alone, tits swollen, ready to nurse

her litter of blind thumbs, slug-toes
of the garbage pile. She did not move

when I rolled her over with the club face
but lay there breathing deeply, heavy

in fear, a pulsating potato, hind foot
chewed away. Golf balls, one after

another, sailed through the air, my swing
improving as they bounced from headstone

to headstone like a giant pinball machine.
I stood staring at the moisture and dirt on her nose,

her breath flaming out, heaved
into what she knows of darkness.

Lake Lure

I dream of sitting in an Adirondack chair in North Carolina
on a cabin porch near Asheville on a three-tiered deck

of *Ipe* wood, overlooking a shadowed valley of mountains
beyond the tree-line. There will be marble floors and Oriental rugs

cushioning the main room and granite counters in the kitchen,
two dishwashers, a *Sub-Zero* fridge and a *Viking* range and oven.

The hand-crafted pantry will be organized, full of *Mason* jars
and garden vegetables. I want ten acres of land

for the driveway winding through the black walnut grove,
a lawn rolling uphill like a graceful green wave

lunging to the front porch where a welcome mat waits
for no one. No strangers will randomly ring my doorbell,

no pop-in relatives,or college kids selling magazines,
only invited guests may swim in the heated pool

or walk with me through the Catawba woods
to the creek where we might fish

or splash around or skip rocks. We will pick wild onions
and lay out a blanket for a picnic, and there will be dogs,

black Labs or Australian shepherds, quick and smart
in case a bear or mountain lion smells the fried chicken

and Mulligatawny. There will be guest rooms
and a finished basement for 9-ball and poker.

When the kids visit, the mud room will be handy
after a rainy day of flag football, and I will have a study

with a chess set and comfortable chairs
and music drifting like mist from room to room: Nick Lowe,

Natalie Cole, or Dave Brubeck, and a Ben Franklin stove
for December nights when you walk around in flannel pj's

and boiled-wool slippers. I will paint the walls
your favorite color. I will shampoo your hair each morning.

The master bedroom will have a walk-in closet
where brevity is the soul of lingerie.

And you, next to me, in another Adirondack chair
will watch Manitoban Elk graze near the *krummholz*

as we sip a *Schloss Doephen* chardonnay
and talk of Michelangelo. There will be a wrought-iron gate

at the foot of the driveway and a wall of bookshelves in the den
for all the poetry the world would like to print.

Ownership

Strange, that's how it felt, each time a realtor's late night call
scattered my parents in a frenzy to pick up dirty clothes,

a week's worth of toys so Ward and June Cleaver
could saunter through our house, staring at all the nice things

we didn't have. We were minimalists by default.
The house didn't sell that winter. Or in the spring.

Somehow it seemed our fault this house wasn't right
for anyone. But this isn't about the old house, it's about the future

we don't know is standing before us, like Jenny's older sister
stripping off her blue one-piece that summer between sixth

and seventh grade after running through the sprinklers, coaxing me
into her bedroom, her dark V frozen before me. "Don't tell anyone,"

she said. And there they were, her breasts, and the rest of her body,
glistening marble. Then she said it was my turn.

I was nothing but a piglet of nakedness
and ran home through an electrical storm of fright.

The next day, Vincent and I cornered a wolverine
eating trash from an oil barrel. Believing we stood a chance

we waited with sticks, but the beast barely turned
his head toward us, crawling off full of bravado.

We stood powerless, transfigured. That night
in a room where a stranger would soon snore, I thought,

how, because we had cornered such an animal,
it somehow belonged to us.

The *Uncertainty Principle*

The great lull of my childhood stretched out
into late summer afternoons, fading
off the glint of Lake Erie so that what was
was no longer, and what I thought
I knew of the universe, I didn't know, how
the more something exists, the less
it is there. And after the sun closed
down the day, as dinner plates were washed
and carefully placed in the cupboards,
there was the inevitable loneliness,
a worried state I felt inside
our rented house, that nothing belonged
to us that couldn't be taken away.

Fast forward twenty years
to a crowded restaurant, where maybe
I imagined what I wanted to hear
while sitting at a small table
with fine white linen, her tongue rolling
a dry chardonnay behind a smile.
There was the clank of a dish, laughter
a few tables over, a door opening
and a car horn stretching through. Right there,
among these sounds, she said she could have married me.
Even if the moon is hidden behind the clouds,
it is there. Still, somehow, it doesn't seem real,
and now she has faded far into oblivion,
which is the antithesis of all I know to be true.

Thomas Merton, Womanizer, Contemplates Our Future

If I never become what I am
meant to be, but always remain
what I am not,
I shall spend eternity
contradicting myself
by being, at once, something
and nothing,
a life that wants
to live but is dead,
a death
that wants to be
dead
but cannot achieve
its own death
because
it still must exist.

Sister Mary Armageddon Teaches Her Students to Hold a Grudge at Saint John of the Impossible Elementary School on 7th Street

The day after Easter I had a test at the hospital
to see what was wrong with me.
Sister Mary A-Bomb couldn't understand why

I could not sit still in class or how
I could read a 4th grade history book
in thirty minutes—then from memory

I recited passages, line by line, from any page
until she was so pissed off, she slapped me
off my chair, saying, "Something's wrong

with you!" which I believed
stemmed from an incident at lunch
the previous week. While eating my pb&j

and sipping chocolate milk,
I beat her at chess.
For a small town, you'd think

I might have at least bumped into her
at some point over the years: the grocery store,
an evening Little League game, Andrews' Greenhouse,

maybe a 4th of July parade, yet, I never did.
Yesterday, in the obits, there she was
with a smile unlike any smile

I ever saw her with, and somehow
she looked nicer than I remember,
preceded in death by a husband

and three children killed in a boating accident
on Lake Erie north of Presque Isle in late July
a few years before becoming a nun.

Skating on Maud's Pond

In eighth grade, everyone started calling me Tex,
a pretty cool nickname for a new kid

which made me feel like one of the guys
when kids I didn't know yelled out my name

in the hall when changing classes or picked me
for dodge ball, because having a guy named Tex

on your team guaranteed a win. It was a lock,
and being popular was like being the *Rhinestone Cowboy*:

a goat-roper in cheap leather boots
kicking back in comfort on a clapboard porch,

legs propped on a white railing, a beat-up six-string plucked
and casting a mellow Glen Campbell tune

across the front yard for the neighborhood girls.
This was Chicago where I could change into my new self

and be the person I thought I wanted to be. Walking home
from school, Ivo and I saw a man kiss a train

after his wife discovered his other family in Utah.
Working as an engineer, he rode the *California Zephyr*

back and forth weeks at a stretch. He knew all the neighbor kids
by name in each city and everyone called him *Uncle Charlie*

the obit said. A couple months later, Ivo and I watched
another man bury a briefcase under a rusted train trestle.

That night we snuck out to dig it up. Drugs.
His dad called the cops—a week later

there was a hit near *Landsman's Pharmacy*.
We swore it was the same guy. Nothing changed,

I was still *Tex*, a kid who'd never ridden a horse or lassoed
any significant memory from childhood, a fantasy

combination of Bret Maverick and Marshall Dillon
with nothing more under my belt than a rustle in the dust

with my cousin over some *Baby Ruth* candy bars.
It's who I needed to be at the time.

The neighborhood girls thought it was cool
how Ivo and I rode to the police station

to give a statement. Donna liked Paul Simon songs,
especially "50 Ways to Leave Your Lover"—singing it

all the time on the bicycle path. In Arlene's basement
Donna let me feel her up and I thought I should have done it

with her then but I wasn't sure if she really wanted to
so we didn't. Ivo was upstairs in Arlene's room, scared,

and ran when Arlene's mom came home early.
Climbing down the trellis, he fell into a snow drift.

I laughed. Next time for sure, we decided. After six months
I hated the name Tex and struggled to change it back.

Dad played a lot of golf that year, finally had a good job
but that wasn't enough to curb a resumé of blown opportunities.

During an argument over money, he smacked mom
around in the kitchen one night as I watched

Efrem Zimbalist, Jr. wrestle a guy on the hood of his car,
gun-metal glint and gold badge flashing in the man's face.

That weekend I found out we were moving. Again. Better job.
Adventure. I'd have to find another nickname

for my new friends. All I wanted now was to be in the F.B.I.,
wrestle the past into submission, make it change into a gentleman

who would never hit a woman or come home drunk
on a kid's birthday, those feelings of loss

and abandonment, as shrill and lovely as Iris Dement
crying about her town and how nothing lasts

so you might as well leave without saying good-bye.
A week before moving south, Ivo and I took the girls skating

on Maud's Pond. I bought Donna a hot chocolate
and sat with her in the ice house to warm her hands.

I'm not sure if she was in love with me
or Tex or what she figured the future might hold,

but I was the boy sitting there rubbing her hands
and blowing warm air into her cupped fingers.

On a dare, Arlene swiped a six-pack of *Huber Bock*
from the *Jewell-Osco*, a five-finger discount

for love. We couldn't go back to her house
because her retarded uncle was visiting from Des Moines

but Donna's mom was at the movies.
Arlene and Ivo did it in Donna's room.

We were in her mother's bedroom.
The blood scared both of us.

On the walk home, Ivo and I didn't say much
and at the corner we split directions—his house

one way toward the shopping center,
mine a dead-end to the gravel pits. When I came home

there was a shattered dinner plate, tens and twenties
scattered on the kitchen floor like children

looking for a safe place to sleep
on an otherwise perfect night.

First Taste of Salt

I can't apologize
for the history of other men
or the bitterness of love
that lasts twenty years
or the fact that the only poems worth writing
are the ones that destroyed our lives.

In the wilderness, I've learned many things,
such as, animals are satisfied
being themselves, yet, here we are
troubled by what we want to be,
or are not,
while at the same time
a tree gives glory to God
by simply being a tree.

Cleaning out an upstairs closet, I found your letter
pressed inside a book, the musty
smell curled around my body. My dog sniffed the papers
then looked around the room, sniffed again
for what the air would not reveal.
He tilted his head as if to say,
"If you'd like, I can find her for you."

In the sunlight, in the pretty bone yard
of lost dreams, everyone is blind
who does not shut their eyes
to the hollow echoing.
I was the first boy who knew what it was like

to enter your body, to break
the salt wound that never heals.
I, reborn, woke one morning and understood
that leaving you was a mistake
I had to make.

Ten states, seventeen houses, a childhood
that taught me to leave everything behind
with ease—twenty-three years later, on my second go-round,
my boys ask questions, curious about their first mother
who could have been. I've told them only
good stories. The quarrel with myself is me,
those experiences reserved for the parched dunes
of being unknown to God,
which is too much privacy for any man.

One night, lost and stumbling
around in the Allegheny Mountains, to keep warm,
I burned crushed coal dust
and pig fat, ate a cup of wild berries,
and thought of you, how in the shower,
the water rolls down your body, cleanses
your feet, and drafts into the drain,
and in time, finds its way to my bathtub,
to me, and the penance
I can't wash away.

III. Family Matters

I've been thinking: This is what the living do...

... I am living. I remember you.

—Marie Howe

The Big Cat Tracks My Grandfather

Sitting on the back porch in an Adirondack chair
with a glass of *Ferrari-Carano* chardonnay circling
and swirling under my tongue, I am bundled
in a wool mountain sweater thick as memory,
such as, one afternoon, with smoke hovering
from my grandfather's *Winstons*, between battles
of *Pinochle* and *Cribbage* at the kitchen table,
he shaved off a few tales of the old life,
how hunting once into the late afternoon
with dusk falling around him, he felt,
then saw, a big cat tracking him from a snowy ridge.

It had been a blustery day, no deer
in sight, nothing (not even a squirrel)
to drag through the woods
to his blue station wagon.

It's the same type of day this afternoon
where beyond the tree-line
on my sixty acres something stirs,
something I cannot see
or know what, but feel moving around me.
A rafter of turkeys is startled
onto my lawn, squawking,
and deeper in the woods, a cry
and then silence.

Scrabble at 8:00 P.M.

Tonight, my son and I argued about the word, *yew*.
It's the twenty-seven points I earned on a cheap triple score
that had him thumbing the dictionary in protest: proper noun
verses your run-of-the-mill tree. He countered,
taking the lead for good with *joker*
and *dogma*, back-to-back like swords clanging
in hard repetition. Then *quiz*, for sixty-three points,
sliced through my *startled* and feeble *house*.

While shifting my tiles around
(an x, 2 u's, 4 i's) he asked if I remembered
standing knee-deep at Myrtle Beach
when an eagle flew directly overhead, wings lumbering
with heavy methodical beats
as a three-foot shark hung in its talons
like a drop tank on a Corsair, mouth slacked open,
staring in disbelief over the horizon.

The words we construct, carefully
or in haste, are used against each other
to win the battle. It's the memories we burn
into our past that bring value, *pocket charms*
against oblivion someone once called it.

Erie, PA 1969: The Night My Father was Pick-Pocketed

My grandfather knew everything
a man should know
who single-handedly defeated the Japs
by sinking all their ships at Guadalcanal.
He never walked away from a barroom brawl,
taking on all comers. With a cock-walk,
there was something in his stride
whereby he earned a free pass
to say whatever he wanted or double park
without care or forethought,
to tell some punks how it was in his day.

It was the city-county rivalry on a grid-iron palace
and we had free tickets
from the cashier at *Save-A-Lot*.
As we entered Veteran's Stadium, a wafting tang
of boiled peanuts and polish sausage snarled my nose.
It was the day before my eighth birthday
and I was amazed so many people cared about football
as though Nixon and Humphrey were stumping in a boxing ring.

Standing room only, my father somehow found a seat for me
next to some pickled strangers. It was, as someone once said,
"loneliness with noise," as my shoulders scrunched

between these onion-smelling men.

Near the end of the fourth quarter, I looked back
to where my father stood cheering,
and saw my grandfather, unmoved,
stoic, a man who had done it all, had seen it all,
and never hesitated to tell me how he could do it all again
with one arm tied behind his back
or how everyone else was doing it wrong.

My Mother Almost Becomes Friends
   with Ann-Margret

For nearly ten hours my mother stood in the August sun,
the line stretching down the block around Graceland

to view Elvis lying-in-state. She waited with her friend
who, the following year would shoot herself

and her daughter. It wasn't jumpsuit-Elvis
or black leather jacket *Jailhouse Rock*-Elvis,

or Elvis making a comeback from Hawaii.
It was pink *Cadillac* and Ed Sullivan-Elvis

my mother said, *clean-cut, like a mannequin
in a white tuxedo.* For years I wondered why

her friend killed herself. Now I know—revenge—how
she could take something away from her husband

and at the same time give him all the world had to offer
in grief. Earlier that spring, I wrote a letter to Elvis

inviting him to Sunday dinner, and now my mother
stood in line to view his casket,

two seconds per person then out a side door
into the wavering heat and news cameras.

Before she walked through the foyer,
my mother saw Ann-Margret sitting

at the bottom of the stairs, roped off, looking up
to make eye contact. She'd been crying,

squeezed inside herself a grief only a lover
or mother can know. I wonder if at that precise moment

had my mother taken Ann-Margret by the hand
and led her into the kitchen

maybe they would have sat at the table and talked,
or perhaps, sat quietly together, strangers

but not strangers, brought together for one moment
by heartache. Drinking coffee and crying,

my mother would have held Ann-Margret's hands
across the oilcloth tabletop.

Maybe they would have become friends
and she would've called my mother occasionally

to say hello from Hollywood, to ask about her life
and children, her dreams. It *was* Ann-Margret

sitting on the bottom of the steps, not the sex-kitten Swede
in black leotards and a tight sweater, gritting her teeth

and giving a coy wink as some photographer strafes
a roll of film. It was Ann-Margret, arms wrapped

around her knees, fingers locked and breath-heavy,
navy blue sweater and pearl necklace

my mother said Elvis had probably given her
one night after a show in Vegas. Maybe

my mother would have stayed at Graceland
for the rest of the day, tidied up around the place,

made lunch for friends and family, washed the dishes
by hand. Whatever was needed.

All of this took no more than a second,
then my mother's friend said, "It's your turn to go."

Jon, Age Eleven

My wife and I took turns at the hospital, day shift,
night shift, watching our son fade
in and out of a bacteria fever
swirling through his blood
as the infection settled in his left ankle.
Two days before, a boy at *Paideia* died from the same thing
though the doctors tried keeping this from us.

Between sleep and hunger binges, we watched movies,
played cards, laughed, and then
the doctor drove a needle through his bone
like a miner setting a dynamite charge
to blow the side off a mountain.

Word got out,
and when the famous soccer player visited
it was like a movie scene where the sick boy smiles
because his hero has shown up. Then he dies happy.
But my son did not die and the virus was contained.
On the way home, we dropped by the *Game Stop*
then *Starbucks*, while across town, a mother
and father stood over a casket being lowered down.

The Last House on the Left

This afternoon my daughter wanted fake blood
and broken pumpkins but opted for goblins

and rubber bats hanging from the flag pole
as she decorated the front door for Halloween—

competing for the scariest house in the neighborhood.
She wrapped a ring of caution tape around the pillars,

slowly crossing the doorway like a murder scene.
Wired skulls and gravestones glowed along the sidewalk.

She weaved bags of cobwebs across the bushes so exacting
it reminded me of a girl I dated in college, how when cleaning

her apartment, she dusted the blue items first,
so intent on perfection and making no mistake,

it had to be the haunting remnants of her mother's ghost
forever driving men away. And now,

my daughter is as purposeful in her actions,
to be so scary everyone will be frightened to ring our door bell

begging for *Almond Joys, Reese's Pieces*, or *Nerds*.
I helped thumbtack threads from the porch ceiling,

what she could not reach with a ladder, spiders
and ghouls hanging down to our faces, balancing

between wanting to help and not interfering. This year
she's dressing up like Sandy from *The Pink Ladies*.

Standing back in the street, she wanted to know if it was scary.
It was scary, in all its beauty. And I told her so.

Skating on Chautauqua Lake, 1920s

When my mother was seventeen her mother died,
and years later, on Monday nights,
alone on the sofa while my father worked
a punch-press at the machine shop, she sat in the dark
with a cup of coffee and a *Marlboro Long*,
trimming off a slow burn.
On t.v., Miss McGillicuddy stuffed chocolates in her bra
as the assembly line sped up. From down the hall,
like an emissary for the *Nielsen Ratings,* I spied the red hair,
heard the scatter-brained caterwauling through the blue cloud
of childhood lingering above my mother. *I Love Lucy*
echoed a deep, quiet pain into the evening.

Each Tuesday morning at breakfast
(forgetting she told the same story last week)
my mother regaled us about her mother
lending a pair of ice skates to Lucille—
how, laughing, they skated away
from the ice house on Chautauqua Lake, toward
the men fishing in shanties—two pretty girls.

My Grandfather's Christmas Tree

Stopping by my grandfather's house for a snowball fight
and some chicken noodle soup, I helped him
carefully place ornaments in tiny boxes
and wound the lights around my arm,
tucking everything in a larger box
then into the attic. My grandmother
was at the mall returning her new vacuum
when my grandfather shoved the Christmas tree
up the fireplace, just jammed it straight up there
with my father's help
because, as he said, "By God,
Christmas ended at midnight!" He struck the match.
When flames shot out the chimney, twenty feet
into the air, I knew we were in trouble.
After the fire department put out the fire,
I remember my grandmother's face looking out
from behind the windshield, her red Mercury
slow-coasting into the driveway, my father's hands
tightening on my shoulders.

When the Bowling Ball Flew Through the T.V.

It was a Christmas story my father sometimes told
                                  in the middle of the summer
after a few beers
about an argument
between his mother and father.

I was now old enough to understand
why it was we moved so often,
a job offer, the need for a new life, just something better
than what we had. . .
                       . . . because about the time we felt comfortable
in school or with the neighbors, there was an itch
to leave nostalgia behind.

I can imagine my grandfather chasing her around the kitchen table,
running through the house, out the back door
then down the driveway to the street,
                   and my grandfather
snapping his belt through the loops
of his gray trousers, half-winding it around his fist—
then the beating my grandmother endured
                                in front of the neighbors
before being dragged through the snow, her red hair knuckled-tight
as he struggled not to slip on the ice, lugging her
like a deer out of the woods.

And I can imagine my father and uncle, as little boys, watching
my grandfather as he looked up at the neighbors
                   leaning on their porch railing,
nodding to them, *Merry Christmas*.

Come Fly with Me

My wife stood in the long gray corridor of Hartsfield Airport,
hands on her hips, pissed off as a rattlesnake

stirred up by some stupid teenagers
with sticks. I was happy to see her, excited to tell her

how I had just driven from the airport to our house
and back in fifty-five minutes, certainly a record

of sorts in the racing lore of *Atlanta International*,
how roaring down the interstate at 110 m.p.h.

without my driver's license, I evaded the police
and other drivers, zipped in and out and between

lesser men, *Botox*-moms, *Porsches*, and taxi drivers
who must understand I'm still in love and a damn good driver

with Secret Service and *007*-driving skills
who was in a big-ass hurry

because taxi drivers, too, must have forgotten,
at some time, their identity, abandoned their wives

in an airport terminal to carry the luggage, alone, without her approval,
no consultation of options, dashed out, simply left her

nagging at the check-in counter for being irresponsible
and ruining the vacation, now missing the only flight

out of town for two days to a tropical paradise.
Every man has had to show proof of who he really is

to the man in a Port Authority hat and blue sweater vest,
en route to some destination of pleasure and exotic excess.

What I was looking for was a way to reconnect
with my wife, to sit side-by-side in a beach chair

with a margarita in one hand, and in the other,
her fingers tracing the inside of my palm, tickling,

relaxing as the world buzzes somewhere where we are not.
With my toes deep in the sand and thinking about anything

except the near misses and dirt track maneuvers
and news helicopters pursuing the *blue whaled-SUV*

for the impending crash and pieces of a shattered life,
all those hours of playing *Grand Theft Auto*

and *Pole Position* fused together into one
life-changing moment: I did it all for her.

My Daughter Likes to Fly

I.

My daughter's legs are peppered with bruises
as if I'd beaten her with a leather belt

for sassing back or not cleaning her bedroom.
The size of quarters, she flinches when I lightly press

these leopard marks, making certain it's nothing more
than balance beam scrapes and tumbling mat crashes.

Hello Kitty leotard and *iCarly* hair bows, chalk coughing
off her hands, her instructor hoists my nimble monkey

to *kip up* the uneven bars into a *back hip circle*.
Two spotters do not help me through this angst

as she turns to see if I'm watching
her *straddle back to handstand*.

II.

Just before bedtime, on my king-sized *Sleep Number* mattress
ratcheted up to 100 with an extra space-age cushion

to support years of tennis, moto-cross wrecks, weeks
of high-adventure camping, and two mountain bike landslides,

she asks for an airplane ride. I contort my body
into an awkward C, my crooked spine

pops and twinges as she balances above me,
arms and legs splayed out, flapping.

It's the pain I push through
so she may hang with her old man.

The giggles start as I spin her side-to-side,
her hair raining down like draperies falling from the sky,

suspended, if just for a moment, as we fly
off somewhere together.

A Path to Elk Creek

Driving down the road with the top laid back and Carole King
singing "Smackwater Jack," I visited the old rough ground
of childhood, buried deep and miles away,
where once in a February blizzard we moved
to the shores of Lake Erie.

In spring, my father led us down a dark path
to a small river, breaking his cane
of light against the rocks. He started a fire
of drift wood, lit a *Marlboro*, bent a few ghost stories
around the fog. There was always a boy hanging around
who somehow knew more than he should for his age,
a kid needing a haircut whose neighborhood was worse
than our sidewalks of grime,
where, on a rare occasion, a wild dream escapes.

After my father's stories,
we'd hand-cup water to the fire
then stand on the river bank peeing,
our gold streams crossing en route
to the greatest of all lakes.

Snazzy Pants on Valley Road

Thinking they were helping out, my grandparents took me shopping
at *Sunshine Department Store*, a discount joint
where, three pairs of plaid slacks later, I was ready
for a new high school, as groovy-looking as Johnny Miller
blasting out of a sand trap at Oakmont. All I wanted were jeans
and sneakers, but my grandfather thought a pair
of white leather *Thom McAn's* with brass buckles would look snazzy—
he'd even spring for engraving my initials on them
in the event they got mixed up in gym class.

I would like to leave it all behind
as though it never happened, the dull ache
of fractured memories and bellbottomed poly-pants
my grandmother called *gentleman's jeans*:
Sansabelt, Farah, Haggar.

If I cannot undo the past, it's up to me
to sort through my inheritance
one leg at a time, a sliced 3-wood into a creek
or high weeds, or a pull-hook
to an all-true recognizable fairway
where we must endure the nicest gestures of love.

In Celebration of Roy Orbison's Birthday

It was a sunny Monday, quite beautiful
by most accounts, the trees bending
and slapping against each other like drunks
trying to steady their drinks. I'd been up since three-thirty,
cracking open the old yearbook like a stone. No consolation.
Then the lights flickered and the computer went blank,
nothing going the way I wanted.
Word stopped responding, like most of the world,
and maybe it was the unified field of everything
here to say, we don't need anymore
of whatever you want to give us.

Then the disc jockey reminded me it was Roy Orbison's birthday,
which brightened me up quite a bit until he played "Crying"
and I began to feel a little sad, worse than rotten
but not quite shitty until he played "Oh, Pretty Woman."
I perked up again and thought of Julia Roberts
and that big friendly smile of hers
and how I bet she gives a great blow job, holding
her hair back with one hand and going to town
on Richard Gere, who someone once told me
I kind of looked like, but not as good.

Then the DJ said Roy Orbison was born in 1936,
the same year as my father, and it dawned on me,

how all these years I've loved Roy's music
but gave my old man so much crap
about every little thing: not exercising, smoking too much,
too much t.v., don't tell me how to hit a golf ball,
watch the cars in front of you, stop bitching about the English
and French being such assholes, stop telling me
the same stories over and over, be nicer to mom,
get over to the table and play *Pinochle*.

And then I realized further, here are two men within months
of being the same age, and yet, one was *over-the-top coolness*
and the other was my father,
and if my dad had been Roy Orbison,
I probably would have hated every song he sang
because yesterday, my thirteen-year-old son called me a moron
and said I was out of shape and needed to make more money.

I realized at that moment, everything
we do or say is shadowed
by a consequence, and much later in life, regret.

Then I remembered what Theroux said,
that ever since childhood,
he had seldom heard a train go by
and not wished to be on it.

Homage: For My Father

The market will not open this morning
and the birds will not fly.
Squeeze all the baseballs into their gloves

and rest them in the closet before grief subsides,
let the beggars beg in the quiet park
where no one walks by, place all the books

upon the shelf to collect an inch of dust.
The bicycle gears will not shift and the cars will not start,
nor will the man on the weather vane twirl his arms.

All the horses will freeze mid-gallop
like bronze statues in a parched field
and tonight the wolves will stop their hunt

so the elk may sleep without concern.
Turn off the television, the water spigot, yield
to all the mind's traffic, disconnect the radio, tell the children

playing in the street to go home. Quiet
the newscaster's microphone, hush
your love-making, please ask the rain not to fall.

I've locked the doors, nailed the windows shut,
snapped the *Tupperware* closed, and sealed the hearth
of all that is unresolved. We know only by unknowing,

we know beyond what there is to say,
whom now will I ask about the world?
The days will continue and coffee pots will perk

in silence as old ladies stand alone in their kitchens
cooking casseroles and making *Jello* with oranges
for today and forever more each bright star

born deep in the universe will have darkness
trailing behind like a boy trying to catch up
to his father on a crowded city sidewalk.

IV. A Tow-Line of Barbed-Wire

I give you back your heart.
I give you permission. . . .

. . . As for me, I am a watercolor.
I wash off.

    —Anne Sexton

The Movie Star's Secret

A man from *Heartland Plumbing* surveyed my postage stamp
of grass this morning, searching for water,
                a modern-day dowser
looking for a leak in the system, any reason
why a million gallons flushed through the pipes
last month to drop a $6,522 bill in my lap.
Like all of us, he searches for the answer, but rarely
finds what he's looking for. He persists, water-witching
                his way through a lonely job, a divining rod
of uncertainty pointing toward the heart of the matter.

God knows
man is alone, a defective
temperament walking the earth forever.
                I followed behind this meter man,
        bending his ear,
kicking up dew as we wedged between the azaleas
and *Steed Hollies*, watching the gauge's nervous jiggle.
I worried he may need to dig up the yard. I realized
my chatter was irritating to this rebel of *Virgula Divina*,
                as Sebastian Münster would call him.
Muck-caked boots on the porch,
inside the house, I channel surfed—until snared
by her lonesome face.

Chicago, late winter 1991, for twenty minutes
I barely noticed the woman cheering for Duke,
until her high-five on a critical Christian Laettner three-pointer,
       and perhaps because I had paid so little attention,
she found me interesting, maybe even attractive, somehow
through platters of potato skins, burgers, and beer,
a happy hour of solitary people laying-over in a snow storm. . .
     . . . but not as isolated as the *Lone Woman of San Nicolas*
who, first discovered in 1853
by an unlikely otter hunter, died just weeks later,
or the *spider-monkey man* choosing
to be left alone, the last survivor
              of his anonymous Brazilian tribe.
      Thirty miles deep, he knows there is no God
in the jungle, no woman
named Eve—he waits for a new journey.

I have been poor and lonely
most of my life, no money for the smallest bauble. . . .
At O'Hare, I'd planned to sleep in the terminal, scrunched up
       with a duffle bag for comfort,
            alone with strangers
claiming a corner or tight angle of wall, a carved-out plot

of relief for the ugly who stare, singular
in laughter for the disaster in their lives.
                        It is loneliness that drives us
to make small talk
because, as Mother Teresa understood
The most terrible poverty
is loneliness.
                    No one will admit
to being alone as they jabber about their hometown
and what waits for them back in Blissville.
        What else do we have to travel on if not faith
that eternity holds the comfort of others
as we struggle
with being lost in the white ruins
of anonymity.

Clapping and cheering college basketball on Sunday,
big-screen t.v.'s scattered throughout
the airport bar, I paid no attention to this woman,
      completely disengaged in the clean, clear lights
of waitresses humping it for a good tip.
            How could I
                or anyone
have recognized the Hollywood glamour through the dark hair,
baseball cap, and rimmed glasses of disguise?

How could any of the world's beautiful people compete
with college basketball? One bar stool away,
she spoke first, casually—"Who're you cheering for?"
                                        . . . Duke, of course.
She was visiting, returning to California
           after her friend's wedding—now a school teacher
in the same high school where they kissed in the library.
She bought the first round of *Hamm's Winter Stock*.

So many years have passed—my withered heart
                                        has a hard time
recognizing that I'm alone anymore—just a natural extension
           of the thickening crust—to most people
I am just a stick,
a thrown rock, kicked away dirt on a shoe—she and I talked.
I never considered anyone would be interested
in anything about me.
                      I think of Octavio Paz
who understood how only man knows he's alone—
                        which must mean the other animals
each think they are a powerful God.

Still, unaware, I asked if we went to school together—
it's possible—I once lived in Chicago
for a few laps around the calendar.

                    I had no idea
she was six months removed from a tabloid divorce,
                laying low
into a quiet life, her new film starting in a month.
What draws people together,
                    some magnet of curiosity?
We like to imagine ourselves being the center
of some universe
where we can be anyone from anywhere
in our imagined lives when traveling to foreign countries
or just across town, the excitement of pretending
to be someone else. . .
                    . . . but the truth is. . . no one knows
or cares who we are.
I was six weeks away from meeting my wife on a blind date.

———

My grandfather walked his backyard with a witch-hazel branch
shaped like a *Y*, gripped loosely in each hand, bent
            as crooked as a politician.
He searched for water
the city told him did not exist—the well had dried
and for more money than God has
            they would connect him at the street.

"Billy-boy, I know there's water here. See this!"
as the divining rods x'ed like magnets over an aquifer
of Biblical proportions.

We rabbit-crossed the backyard, his nagging wife
                    in tow, passed the *McIntosh*
and *Granny Smith* trees, leaf-full and sweet canopy
of drooping fruit hanging on slug branches,
low enough for a boy with a baseball bat.

She dropped a dime to her agent, "I'm staying
one more night," then she whispered in my ear
                    her name—removed her glasses,
ball cap, shook her hair
like some wild thing
                    then quickly back on as her soft breath
brought the marquee lights alive, lifting high
in big Marilyn Monroe letters, the dazzle
and glitter of Rodeo Drive.
Isn't this why we explore the world,
           to find what makes us whole,
              another person to tumble down the hill with?

Two hours from O'Hare,

                        she usually traveled with a bodyguard,
but not at home
            where family laughter echoes from the kitchen,
where she's still her parents' little girl, the unsophisticated
expectations of farm life, how she can walk downstairs
in her flannel pajamas, kiss her mother,
                        scold her father for eating too much bacon.

            Later, in the garage, pumping her bicycle tires
she rides down a gravel road to visit old friends
who work their family farm. Her sisters still tease her,
a perpetual initiation into the club of womanhood—how
she dyed her hair
midnight black for the junior prom. . .
                        . . . to earn money for an acting class
she delivered sixty-four newspapers over rambling back roads
            of cinder stone,
seventeen miles on a second-hand *Huffy*
before quitting after three days.

What was I to do?
I could only smile and laugh
            at my ignorance, because
            I have always been just a man
who needed a marquee sign

the size of the *HOLLYWOOD* billboard

or a woman standing naked in front of me

to understand my next move.

                        I'd seen most of her movies.

She's the kind of woman men desire—

                but fear

talking to—there's no way

to compete with whatever is out there

in her other world, men

with so much money

                it's as if I'm drowning

on a raging river

and the cure for my loneliness is a tow-line

of barbed-wire.

                   ———

At our quiet table she sat with her back to the crowd,

a position of vulnerability—she hadn't been kissed

in more than a year,

                the dark cloud of marriage holding her

inside her Malibu home, retreating

into a quieter world—reading movie scripts

and novels. . . some traveling.

Next morning, after room service,
she asked me
to covet our secret time
together—she did not need any publicity.
    What courage must be drummed up
to curb the desire there is
not to be alone in the world.
        There was a boy in high school
she had a crush on, but now, being famous
it's difficult to call, because what if he's married—how
does his wife with curlers in her hair
    and babies spilling food on the floor
compete with a movie star calling her husband
    . . . if just to say *hello—how've you been doing?*

———

The man from *Heartland Plumbing*
drove a ten-foot metal stake
through the heart of my Bermuda grass, through red clay
and builder-grade land fill, searching
for moisture underground, seepage, but found none.
My grandfather,
never to be misled or cheated, refused
to pay the city. For years

the water petered out of the tap.

———

When she kisses a leading man on-screen, a man
who is tall, with an ivory smile, abs and pecs of Adonis
and hair bouncing in wild abandon, lucid syllables
flowing from his lips,
        does she think of me?

I know a secret,
how an ordinary guy sitting in a Chicago airport bar
can bump into a glamorous Hollywood actress
and forever fold up into a little secret square of memory
everything we have always wanted
to brag about to our buddies,
                      that one of us broke through
to that mysterious island, if just for a moment.

Acknowledgements

Grateful acknowledgement is made to the following journals, whose editors first published these poems:

Agnes Scott College Writers' Festival Magazine: "Hunting Mule Deer"
Calliope: "Skating On Chautauqua Lake, 1920s"
Crack the Spine: "Outside Winn Dixie in Suburban Plaza"
Floodwall: "Feeling Like I'm in a William Holden Movie"
Gulf Stream Literary Magazine: "My Last Fishing Trip"
Harpur Palate: "Spoon River in Uganda," "Elegy for a School Bus Driver"
The Istanbul Review (Turkey): "Ownership"
The James Dickey Review: "When the Bowling Ball Flew Through the T.V."
Mason's Road: "Blackbird"
MOJO: "In Celebration of Roy Orbison's Birthday"
The Moth (Ireland): "Betrayal," "Lake Lure"
Negative Capability Press Anthology of Georgia Poetry: "Outside Winn Dixie in Suburban Plaza"
The North American Review: "Hero With a Thousand Faces"
Owen Wister Review: "Friday, Before Dusk"
Rattle: "The Old Me," "The Movie Star's Secret"
Southern Poetry Anthology Volume V: Georgia: "My Grandfather's Christmas Tree"
Teesta Rangeet (India): "The Uncertainty Principle"
Valparaiso Poetry Review: "The Big Cat Tracks My Grandfather," "Homage: For My Father"
Verdad: A Journal of Literature & Art: "Sister Mary Armageddon Teaches Her Students to Hold a Grudge at Saint John of the Impossible Elementary School on 7th Street"
Wilderness House Literature Review: "Jon, Age Eleven," "Erie, PA 1969: The Night My Father was Pick-Pocketed"

Notes

The James Dickey quote is from "Cherry Log Road," first published in *Helmets* (1964).

"Hunting Mule Deer": This story originated from an old tale I first heard from Grant Teaff, legendary football coach at Baylor University.

"Reading from the *Portuguese* in Atikokan": This is a reference to *Sonnets from the Portuguese* by Elizabeth Barrett Browning between 1845–1846 and published in 1850.

The characters, Stan and Iris, in "Thoughts During a Thunderstorm: Montana" derive from Beth Gylys' poem "Alone, Open Road," from *Spot In the Dark* (2004).

"The Old Me": This was highly influenced by Everett Maddox's "Tick Tock" from his *Selected Poems* (2009), edited by Ralph Adamo.

"Feeling Like I'm in a William Holden Movie": On December 6, 1917 in the Halifax Harbor, the SS Mont-Blanc, a French cargo ship containing wartime explosives, ignited after colliding with the Norwegian SS Imo. The explosion killed more than 2,000 people in Halifax from collapsing buildings, fires, and debris from the blast, especially glass from the windows. It was the largest man-made explosion until the invention of the atomic bomb.

"My Last Fishing Trip": Charlie Rich (1932–1995) started out as a session musician for Sun Records in Memphis. He was an award-winning country star best known for his #1 hits, "Behind Closed Doors" and "The Most Beautiful Girl."

The title *"Hero With a Thousand Faces"* is borrowed from Joseph Campbell's 1949 book of the same title. George Barris was an American photographer who photographed many Hollywood stars, including many iconic photos of Marilyn Monroe. On July 13, 1962, Barris took the last photograph of Marilyn Monroe.

"*Spoon River* in Uganda" is a reference to Edgar Lee Master's 1916 collection of poems, *Spoon River Anthology*.

The quote from James Wright is from "Having Lost My Sons, I Confront the Wreckage of the Moon: Christmas, 1960" originally published in *The Branch Will Not Break* (1963).

"The *Uncertainty Principle*": The *Uncertainty Principle*, per Andrew Zimmerman Jones and Daniel Robbins, was discovered by Werner Heisenberg who stated, ". . . the more precisely you measure one quantity, the less precisely you can know another associated quantity. The quantities sometimes come in set pairs that can't both be completely measured."

"Elegy for a School Bus Driver": Vida Blue, 3-time World Series winner (1972, 1973, and 1974), as well as a 6-time All-Star, won the American League Cy Young Award and Most Valuable Player Award in 1971. He pitched for the Athletics, the Giants, and the Royals.

"Thomas Merton, Womanizer, Contemplates Our Future": The contents of this poem originate from Merton's *New Seeds of Contemplation* (1961).

The quote from Marie Howe is from "What the Living Do" originally published in *What the Living Do* (1998).

"*Scrabble* at 8:00 P.M.": The quote, "*pocket charms/against oblivion*" is from David Bottoms' poem, "Easter Shoe Epistle," first published in *Waltzing Through the Endtime* (2004).

"Erie, PA 1969: The Night My Father was Pick-Pocketed": The quote, "loneliness with noise" is from William Matthews' poem, "Cheap Seats, The Cincinnati Gardens, Professional Basketball, 1959," from *Time & Money: New Poems* (1996).

"The Last House On the Left": This title refers to the 1972 horror film directed by Wes Craven.

"Skating On Chautauqua Lake, 1920s": My grandmother, Florence Card (née LeBaron) grew up in Celeron, NY and was a childhood friend of Lucille Ball.

"Come Fly with Me" is the 1958 title track of Frank Sinatra's album by the same name. It was composed by Jimmy Van Heusen with lyrics by Sammy Cahn. This song was also sung by Frankie Avalon in the 1963 film, *Come Fly with Me.*

"Snazzy Pants on Valley Road": Johnny Miller is an American golfer who won two major titles—the 1973 U.S. Open and the 1976 British Open. He was the first golfer to shoot a 63 in a major championship, which he accomplished in the final round to win the U.S. Open.

"In Celebration of Roy Orbison's Birthday": Roy Orbison (1936-1988) is known for his rock'n'roll hits "Oh, Pretty Woman," "Crying," "Only the Lonely," "Dream Baby," and "Blue Bayou." He was also a member of The Traveling Wilburys. Paul Theroux stated in his 1975 travelogue, "The Great Indian Railway Bazar," "I have seldom heard a train go by and not wished I was on it."

The quote from Anne Sexton is from her poem, "For My Lover, Returning to His Wife," published in *Love Poems* (1969).

About the Author

William Walsh is originally from Jamestown, New York, but has lived throughout the United States. He lives with his wife and three children in Atlanta. His books include *Speak So I Shall Know Thee: Interviews with Southern Writers*, *The Ordinary Life of a Sculptor*, *The Conscience of My Other Being*, *Under the Rock Umbrella: Contemporary American Poets from 1951-1977*, and *David Bottoms: Critical Essays and Interviews*. His work has appeared in the *AWP Chronicle*, *Cimarron Review*, *Five Points*, *Flannery O'Connor Review*, *The Georgia Review*, *James Dickey Review*, *The Kenyon Review*, *Michigan Quarterly Review*, *North American Review*, *Poetry Daily*, *Poets & Writers*, *Rattle*, *Shenandoah*, *Slant*, the *Valparaiso Poetry Review*, and others. His interviews, which have been published in over fifty journals, include Czeslaw Milosz, Joseph Brodsky, A.R. Ammons, Doris Betts, Fred Chappell, Pat Conroy, Harry Crews, James Dickey, Mary Hood, Madison Jones, Donald Justice, Lee Smith, Ariel Dorfman, Rita Dove, Eamon Grennan, Ursula Leguin, Andrew Lytle, Marion Montgomery, and many more. He is currently completing his PhD at Georgia State University. His website is www.thepigrider.com, named after his forthcoming novel, *The Pig Rider*.